Nihil Obstat: Fr. Philip-Michael F. Tangorra, S.T.L.
Censor Librorum
Imprimatur: + Most Rev. Arthur J. Serratelli, S.T.D., S.S.L., D.D.
Bishop of Paterson
December 26, 2015

Text © 2016 by THE REGINA PRESS
an imprint of Catholic Book Publishing Corp.
77 West End Road
Totowa, NJ 07512

Illustrations: Marifé González
Illustrations © SUSAETA EDICIONES, S.A.

(RG14652)

ISBN: 978-0-88271-399-1   CPSIA February 2016 10 9 8 7 6 5 4 3 2 1 S/S

Printed in India
www.catholicbookpublishing.com

Prayers to My Guardian Angel

Regina Press

MY GUARDIAN ANGEL

MY Angel guards me and watches over me. My Angel helps to protect me.

Under my Angel's care, I feel safe. I pray often to my ever-watchful Angel.

WHEN I WAKE

DEAR Angel, take my hand. Help me think about, speak about, and do only those things that are pleasing to God.

DURING THE DAY

MY heavenly Angel, be with me as I thank God Who made the sun, the sky, and the clouds.

Help me to love all that God has made.

MY FAMILY

DEAR Guardian Angel, thank you for showing me how to love my parents and to be kind to my brothers and sisters. I know they are God's gift to me.

And when I disobey my parents or don't get along with my brothers and sisters, show me that I have displeased God. Help me to be sorry.

AT SCHOOL

ANGEL of God, when I am at school, help me to pay attention in class, study hard, obey my teachers, and be kind to my classmates.

While I am on the playground during recess, help me to play fair and make sure no one is left out of the games.

15

I feel that you are right there with me, my Angel, to help me do what I am supposed to do.

Help me to know right from wrong, because that is one of the best lessons I can learn.

WITH MY FRIENDS

DEAR Guardian Angel, as you watch from above while I have fun with my friends, I feel safe.

Help me to be good to my friends, to share with them, and to let them know I care about them.

BEFORE MEALS

MY dear Angel, help me to be grateful for the meals I enjoy with my friends and family.

Help me to know that I am lucky because I have enough food to eat at every meal.

And also help me to remember those who are hungry and to pray for them every day.

MY ACTIVITIES

DEAR Angel, I often am busy with many different things—sports, arts and crafts, the Internet and video games, reading…

With so much to do, sometimes I forget about God. Thank you for helping me to think about Him and all He means to me.

AT BEDTIME

O MY Angel, thank you for being with me and covering me with a blanket of love.

My heart is light as I settle in my bed. With you to protect me, I have nothing to fear.

Sweet Angel, thank you for holding me close between the dark of night and the dawn of day.

I smile to myself in sleep because I know God is in heaven and all is right in my world.

PRAYER TO PRAY BETTER

DEAR Guardian Angel, help me to pray better. Show me how to thank God and to praise Him.

Thank you for your special help that makes it possible for me to tell God how much I love Him.

PRAYER OF APPRECIATION

MY dear Angel,
you help me appreciate
all that God has made.

You help me smell
blooming flowers.

You help me feel
warm sunshine.

Thank you for helping
me to be aware of all
God has created.

ANGELS OF GOD

ANGELS of God,
what a blessing that
you watch over me and
keep me safe from harm,
just as you watched
over the Baby Jesus in the
stable at Bethlehem.

MY ANGEL'S SONG

MY Angel sings a song
that's meant for me to hear.
It's a song of joy and
the words are very clear.

I hear all about Jesus
and all He's done for me.

I'm told how He was born
and lived a life like mine.
But then when He grew up,
He showed us many signs.

He helped the blind to see
and the lame to walk.
And many people listened
whenever He would talk.

Then He died upon a tree
and rose on the third day.
He did this out of love
to take our sins away.

What a song of His love
flowing from heaven above!

GOODNIGHT PRAYER

ANGEL of God,
I pray that you
will watch over me
while I sleep.

I pray that I will be
good and kind like
Jesus Who was a child
like me.

I hope that the love
of Mary, my Mother,
will surround me
as I fall sleep.

I ask that my family
will be blessed
as the gift of today
comes to an end.

I pray the Holy Spirit
will descend upon me
so that I will sleep
in His peace.

I pray that God
will hear my prayers
and know how much
I love Him.

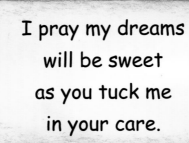

I pray my dreams
will be sweet
as you tuck me
in your care.

Finally, I thank you,
my Guardian Angel,
my companion,
my closest friend,
for staying with me
all the while I sleep.
Goodnight.